TWO BY TWO

Designed and Pieced by

LESLEY BRANKIN

Quilted by

Jan Chandler
(Quilting Solutions)

An intermediate/advanced level project using
Foundation Piecing techniques

CONTENTS

Materials 3
Making up the Blocks 4
Choosing Fabric 4
Assembling the Quilt 5
Inner Sashing 8
Borders 8
Quilting 9
Binding 9
Finishing 9

General Techniques 10
  • Plated Tail
  • Tassel Tail
  • Folded Ears

Foundation Piecing - a Brief Guide 11

	Guidance Notes	Colour Plate	Templates
Bats	13	32	33
Camel	13	31	34
Cat & Mouse	14	28	35
Dog	14	29	36
Dolphin	15	26	37
Dove & Butterfly	15	31	38
Elephant	16	31	39
Fishes	16	26	40
Geese	17	27	41
Giraffe	17	30	42-43
Lion	18	30	44
Lioness	18	30	45
Mrs Noah	19	28	46
Noah & Bees	19	29	47
Penguins	20	27	48
Pig	20	28	49
Polar Bear	21	27	50
Rabbits	21	29	51
Sea Lion	22	27	52
Sheep	22	29	53
Snakes & Snails	23	28	54
Whale	23	26	55
Zebra	24	31	56
Ark Roof	24		

Disclaimer

Every care has been taken to ensure the accuracy of these instructions, but no guarantee can be given with regard to the finished quilt as materials and procedures used will necessarily vary.

MATERIALS

Dimensions: 62" x 87" approx.

This quilt is made from many different fabrics, many used in small quantities. The nature of foundation piecing techniques makes it difficult to give precise fabric requirements so the following are quite generous quantities. Quantities provided assume standard width (112 cm, 42"/44") wide fabrics.

Background, ark and border fabrics:

- 0.6 m (24") pale blue
- 0.25 m (10") blue floral pattern
- 0.3 m (12") pale green
- 0.25 m (10") green grass pattern
- 0.3 m (12") mid green
- 0.3 m (12") green wave
- 0.5 m (20") dark green
- 0.3 m (12") mottled pattern
- 0.5 m (20") mid brown
- 0.3 m (12") pebble pattern
- 0.5 m (20") mid blue
- 0.5 m (20") dark blue
- 0.5 m (20") blue wave
- 0.25 m (10") light brown
- 0.3 m (12") dark brown
- 0.1 m (4") red

Animal Blocks:

- animal prints and fabric scraps*
- background fabrics (included in amounts given above)
- Stitch 'n' Tear or thin paper for paper piecing (e.g. cheap computer paper)
- a variety of ¼" and ⅜" buttons
- perlé embroidery threads

Additional Needs:

- neutral sewing thread
- 0.25 m (12") dark green for inner sashing
- single bed sized piece of wadding
- 70" x 95" backing fabric (allows for Long Arm quilting)
- 1.1 m (42") dark green for double binding
- decorative quilting threads

* If buying fabrics specially, you will need approximately a fat eighth of the main fabric for each animal pair (slightly more for giraffes).

CHOOSING FABRICS

Choosing fabrics is both great fun and a fundamental step to stamping your own identity on any project. Just because I have chosen to use a specific colour or texture of a fabric does not mean that you are obliged to follow my dictate. Use this design as an opportunity to follow your own creative style and perhaps use up some of that ever-growing stash?

For the backgrounds, I would recommend that you use non-patterned fabrics that will not compete with the animals themselves. Plains, marbles or gentle ombres are ideal. The ground cover strips are an ideal chance to indulge in some vibrant or highly patterned designs. Wavy fabrics are great for water; small spots or circles can represent a hard, stony surface and what about including a floral or two as vegetation?

As the animals themselves do not use very much fabric, this offers an 'opportunity' to source specific fabric designs. You may be lucky enough to find some special animal skin prints, however, it is probable that you will have to look for suitable alternatives. Be sure to audition all sorts of patterned and textured fabrics. Does it look like skin, fur, feathers etc. - my lion's mane is actually a pinecone design.

MAKING UP THE BLOCKS

My suggested order of working is to make all the blocks before you start to construct the full quilt top. However, if you prefer you can of course work one row at a time.

Instructions for each block are given individually, this allows you to use the designs simply as quilt blocks and then use them to create your own quilt and project layouts.

All of the blocks use Foundation Piecing techniques. A brief overview of the technique has been included here (see page 11) or there are many excellent texts available explaining this technique if you are not already familiar with it. The important thing to remember is to always to work in the order given (rather like a painting by numbers set) and to press and trim seams as you go. For ease of use when piecing, I strongly recommend that you always work with generous sized pieces of fabric - if you are too miserly you will find that frustration may rule the day! Likewise allow a generous amount of fabric at the edges of the block - that way you will have plenty of scope when trimming your blocks to their final sizes.

If you are making up my full quilt design you will need to make the appropriate number of blocks for each animal. The block instructions tell you how many of that block to make or you can refer to the quilt construction figure on page 6. When making more than one block for each type of animal, you may wish to do as I did and use a mirrored image for some of the blocks. In this case you will need to transpose the given template patterns using a scanner, carbon paper or ask a copy shop to do this for you.

All of the blocks are 6" finished size with the exception of Mrs. Noah, the Giraffes and the Ark's Roof. When trimming your blocks ready to sew together, do make sure they are ½" bigger than the finished size specified. This provides your ¼" seam allowance

ASSEMBLING THE QUILT

A few hints before you start:

- When cutting background strips you may need to join several smaller lengths of fabric together to make the total width specified - the instructions given refer to the total joined length required.
- For ease of working, you may find it easier to cut sashing and strip lengths just slightly longer than needed - these can then be trimmed as you sew.
- Remember to press seam allowances as you proceed.
- The figure overleaf describes the general quilt block layout and should be used as a general reference diagram.

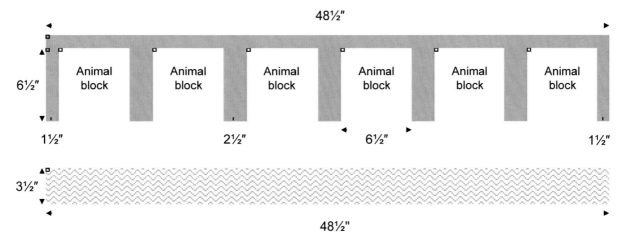

Cutting sizes for spacer strips

Row 1

1. From dark blue fabric cut 6½" strips:
   - 2 x 1½"
   - 5 x 2½"
2. Join strips and animal blocks as shown overleaf.
3. From dark blue fabric cut a 48½" x 1½" wide strip. Attach to top of joined blocks, see figure above.
4. From blue wave fabric cut a 48½" x 3½" wide strip. Attach to bottom of joined blocks, see figure above.

Row 2

Repeat as for Row 1 using mid blue and blue wave fabrics.

Rows 3 and 4 - refer to figure overleaf for block and strip placements

1. From both mid brown fabric and dark green cut 6½" strips:
   - 1 x 1½"
   - 4 x 2½"
2. Join mid brown strips, camel and zebra blocks, narrow strip to left.
3. Join dark green strips, elephant, lion and lioness blocks, narrow strip to left.
4. From mid brown fabric cut a 33½" x 1½" wide strip. Attach to top of camel/zebra section.

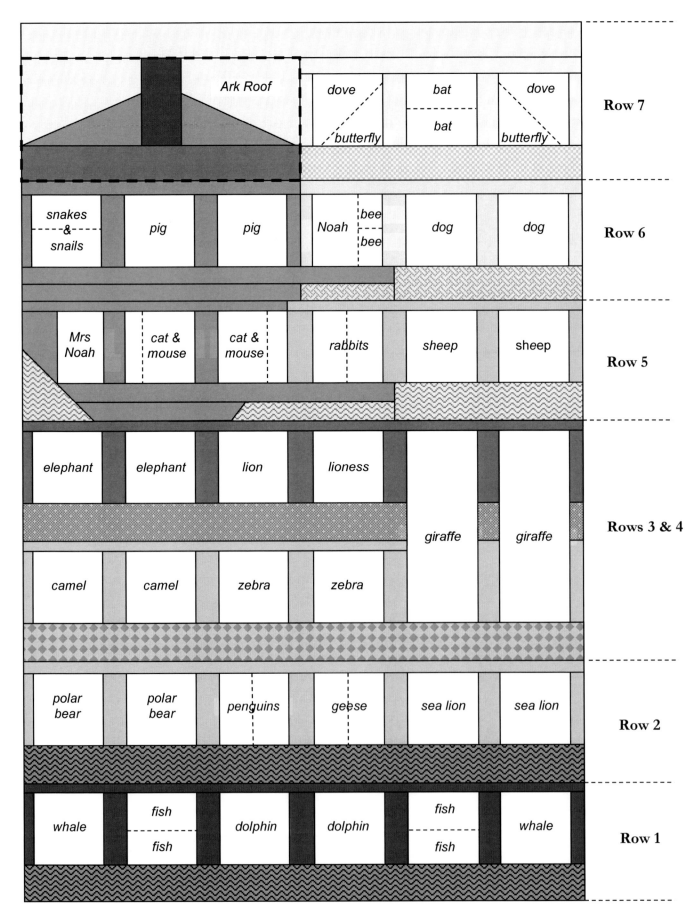

Row 7

Row 6

Row 5

Rows 3 & 4

Row 2

Row 1

Quilt Construction

5. From mottled pattern fabric cut a 33½" x 3½" wide strip. Attach to bottom of elephant/lion section.
6. Join elephant/lion section to top of camel/zebra section.
7. Cut the following:
   - a 2½" x 7½" and a 1½" x 7½" strip from mid brown
   - a 2½" x 3½" and a 1½" x 3½" strip from mottled pattern
   - a 2½" x 6½" and a 1½" x 6½" strip from dark green
8. Join together the wider strips to create a single long vertical stripe, repeat with narrower strips.
9. Join vertical stripes with giraffe blocks, narrow strip to right.
10. Join giraffe section to other animals.
11. From dark green fabric cut a 48½" x 1½" wide strip. Attach to top of joined sections.
12. From pebble pattern fabric cut a 48½" x 3½" wide strip. Attach to bottom of joined sections.

Row 5 - refer to figure opposite for block and strip placements

1. From mid green fabric cut 6½" strips:
   - 1 x 1½"
   - 3 x 2½"
2. Join strips to sheep and rabbit blocks, narrow strip to right.
3. From mid green fabric cut a 25½" x 1½" wide strip. Attach to top of joined sections.
4. From dark brown fabric cut 6½" strips:
   - 1 x 3½"
   - 2 x 2½"
5. Join strips and Mrs. Noah and cat blocks, wider strip to left.
6. From dark brown fabric cut a 23½" x 1½" wide strip. Attach to top of joined sections.
7. Join Mrs Noah/cat section to sheep/ rabbit section.
8. From green wave cut a 16½" x 3½" strip and a 13" x 2" strip.
9. From dark brown cut 2" strips:
   - 1 x 32½"
   - 1 x 20"
10. Join the shorter brown strip to the green wave 2" strip using a 45 degree angled seam.
11. Join to longer brown section (goes on top). Trim if necessary.
12. Attach larger green wave strip and add to bottom of animal section.
13. Cut a 6½" square of green wave fabric. With pencil, mark a diagonal line across the back from top right to bottom left corner.
14. With right sides facing, match bottom left hand corners. Stitch along pencil line. Fold fabric to right side. Trim extra fabric away from back.

Row 6 - refer to figure opposite for block and strip placements

1. From pale green fabric cut 6½" strips:
   - 2 x 1½"
   - 2 x 2½"
2. Join strips and Noah/bees and dog blocks, narrow strips at ends.
3. From pale green fabric cut a 24½" x 1½" wide strip. Attach to top of joined sections.
4. From dark brown fabric cut 6½" strips:
   - 2 x 1½"
   - 2 x 2½"
5. Join strips and snake/snail and pig blocks, narrow strips at ends.
6. From dark brown fabric cut 24½" x 1½" wide strip. Attach to top of joined sections.

7. Join snake/pig section to Noah/dog section.
8. From green grass pattern cut a 16½" x 3½" strip and an 8½" x 2" strip.
9. From dark brown cut 2" strips:
    - 1 x 32½"
    - 1 x 24½"
10. Join short brown strip to short green grass pattern strip.
11. Join to longer brown section (goes on top).
12. Attach to larger green grass pattern strip and then add to bottom of animal so that centre line matches.

Row 7 - refer to figure on page 6 for block and strip placements

1. From pale blue fabric cut 6½" strips:
    - 2 x 1½"
    - 2 x 2½"
2. Join strips and dove/butterfly and bat blocks, narrow strips at ends.
3. From pale blue fabric cut a 24½" x 1½" wide strip. Attach to top of joined sections.
4. From blue floral pattern fabric cut a 24½" x 3½" wide strip. Attach to bottom.
5. Join dove/bat section to Ark Roof block.
6. From pale blue fabric cut a 48½" x 3½" wide strip. Attach to top of joined sections.

Joining the Rows

1. Using the figure on page 6 as a guide join the rows together in the order shown.
2. Measure your quilt top; it should be a 48½" x 73½" rectangle.

INNER SASHING

1. From dark green fabric cut 2, 1½" strips totalling 73½" and 2 totalling 50½" in length (you will probably need to join smaller lengths).
2. Sew longer strips onto each side of quilt.
3. Sew shorter strips to top and bottom of quilt.

BORDERS

1. From left over fabrics cut 86 rectangles of fabric, each measuring 6¼" x 3½" and 4 measuring 6¼" x 4¼" (for the corners). My border is made from sequenced background fabrics but you could include animal prints or use a random selection, depending on what fabrics you have left.
2. Join rectangles together (longer sides together) to make border strips:
    - 2 x 25 rectangles for sides
    - 2 x 18 rectangles for top and bottom, plus 1 wider rectangle each end
3. Sew longer strips onto each side of quilt.
4. Sew shorter strips to top and bottom of quilt.

QUILTING

1. Prepare the quilt sandwich. If you plan to have your quilting done on a Long Arm machine ensure that your backing is at least 3" larger all round than your quilt top (i.e. at least 68" x 93") or size requested by your machinist.
2. Baste and quilt according to your personal preference.

Two by Two was custom long arm quilted. The outside edges of the animals and ark, plus the main background seams were 'stitched in the ditch'. The background to each row was then quilted using flowing, free motion designs, complimenting the animals and fabrics used. The individual animals were not quilted, allowing them to 'stand forward' of the background.

> *If your quilt is for a child, do not add button eyes, thread tails etc. that can be easily removed. Consider adding quilted tails and eyes instead.*

The border was simply quilted using a single cross-hatch across each rectangle. Appropriate variegated threads were used with a complimentary colour on the back.

BINDING

1. Trim all sides of quilt so that layers are even and corners are square.
2. My quilt is edged with a 1" double binding. Cut sufficient 5" wide strips of fabric such that, when joined, they will go around the edge of the quilt, plus about 10" extra in length.
3. Join all strips together on the diagonal to make a single long strip.
4. Fold binding strip in half along the entire length, right sides outermost. Press.
5. Fold in ¼" along length of open long edge (both layers together). Press
6. Starting at centre of bottom edge and with right sides together, pin binding in place so that the ¼" fold line lies 1" in from the edge (you may find it useful to mark this line). Pin in place. Machine stitch along this fold line until 1" from the corner. Backstitch a little and remove quilt from the machine. Fold the binding strip up at 45° and then back down such that the ¼" fold line now lies 1" in from the next quilt edge. This gives spare fabric to fold over to the back of the quilt, ensuring neat corners.
7. Stitch along fold line, starting from top edge and thereby holding the mitre fold in place as you sew.
8. Continue sewing down the binding strip and forming corners until you return to the start. Fold in overlap edges to form a neat ending. Slip stitch down.
9. Fold the binding to the back of the quilt, carefully easing out fullness at corners. Pin.
10. Hem along the seam line. Sew down mitred corners.

FINISHING

1. Add button eyes and embroider appropriate tails, features etc. as indicated in the relevant block instructions.
2. Don't forget to add that all-important label.

> *Bask in the undoubted admiration that your quilt will bring!*

GENERAL TECHNIQUES

Plaited Tail

Take 6 strands of perlé thread, each about 7" long. Fold in half and stitch centre fold firmly to animal's bottom. Divide the strands into three and plait for a length of about 2", knot end securely and trim. The tail can either be left to hang free or stitched down.

Tassel Tail

Take 4 strands of perlé thread, each about 8" long. Fold in half and stitch centre fold firmly to the respective animal's bottom. Now wind the attaching thread round the tail to bind individual strands together. Knot. Trim ends evenly.

Folded Ears

To make an ear, take a square of chosen 'ear' fabric.

Fold in half, press.

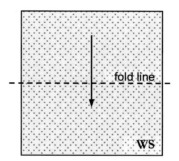

With fold to the top, take one of the top corners of the rectangle to the middle of the bottom side.

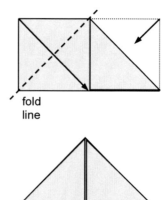

Repeat, press.

Prairie Point

Slip the resultant triangle (called a prairie point) into the associated seam, right sides facing downwards and pointing in opposite direction to its final position. Adjust to give a good-proportioned/positioned ear for the animal.

When you have stitched along the associated seam, trim and remove any excess bulk. After the block is finished, fold the ear into its final position and press. Optionally add a small stitch to hold the tip in place.

FOUNDATION PIECING - A BRIEF GUIDE

Foundation Piecing, also known variously as 'Paper Piecing' and the 'Stitch and Flip Technique', is a very accurate piecing technique where fabric patches are stitched to the reverse of a foundation block or unit (part of a block). Depending on the material used for the foundation, this can be either left permanently in place (e.g. lightweight cotton fabric or sew-in interfacing) or can be removed (e.g. paper or Stitch 'n' Tear).

The advantages of Foundation Piecing over the use of traditional piecing or template methods is that it allows you greater scope to piece more intricate designs. It can also be very quick to work once you become familiar with the technique.

Materials

You will need:

- Foundation paper, Stitch 'n' Tear or fine fabric e.g. calico or lawn
- Cottons or other fine fabrics e.g. silk
- Neutral coloured sewing thread

General Method

Patches are stitched to the blank side of the foundation. As such it is useful to have acccss to a light source (e.g. window or light box) to help position patches. Seam allowances are trimmed to size as the block is stitched so accurate cutting of the pieces is not necessary. When machine stitching, remember to use a slightly smaller stitch than usual especially if the foundation is to be removed.

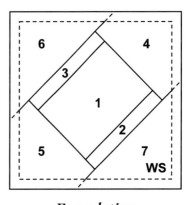

First the block or unit design must be traced or photocopied accurately on to the foundation and the order of stitching each patch noted. The design should appear in reverse to that of the finished block or unit.

Foundation Template

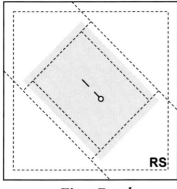

First Patch

Begin with the patch for area 1. Cut a piece of fabric slightly larger than the area to be covered and position this right side up, onto the blank side of the foundation covering area 1. Pin in place.

Next cut a piece of fabric that generously covers area 2. Place this right side down over patch 1, aligning the corresponding allowance edge. To help with placement of fabric, mark each end of the stitching line with a pin. Pin patch 2. Turn the foundation over and stitch along the line between patch 1 and 2 starting and finishing a few stitches beyond the marked line.

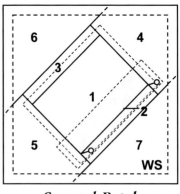

Second Patch

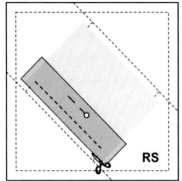

Trim Fabric Allowance

Turn unit over and trim seam allowances.

Flip patch 2 so that the right side of the fabric is now visible and press flat.

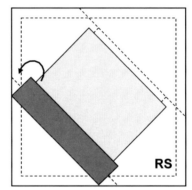

Flip and Press

Trim unit allowance to ¼"

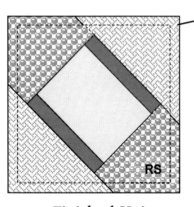

Finished Unit

Continue to stitch patches in numerical order, making sure that the fabric extends over the seam allowance around the outer edge of the unit. When the unit is complete, trim back seam allowances to a neat ¼".

Sewing Units Together

Units are sewn together with a ¼" seam allowance as they would be for any traditionally pieced patchwork technique. If units are different shapes then follow the construction order given in the instructions.

Papers need to be removed - this can be done once a unit has been trimmed to its accurate size or it can be done after units have been joined.

Fabric foundations can be left in if desired.

BATS

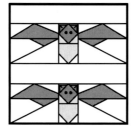

Block Size: 6" x 6" (make 1)

You will need:

- background - pale blue
- bats - 2 shades brown
- buttons - 4 x ¼" black

Making a Block

1. Make two copies of foundation Units A through C.
2. Using 1½" fabric squares make 4 small *folded ears*.
3. Foundation piece both Units A using pale blue for background.
4. When adding patches 7s and 8s, remember to insert a prairie point within each associated seam.
5. Foundation piece Units B and C using pale blue for background.
6. Referring to Unit Placement diagram, join a Unit B and a Unit C to either side of both Units A.

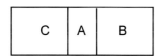

Bat Sub Unit

7. Cut two 6½" x 1½" strip of sky fabric (Unit D) and sew one to top of each bat block.
8. Join the two bat blocks together:

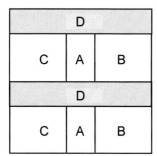

Unit Placement
(right sides facing)

9. Remove papers.

Finishing (completed after quilting)

1. Sew on buttons for eyes.

CAMEL

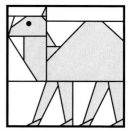

Block Size: 6" x 6" (make 2)

You will need:

- background - mid brown
- camel - sand
- buttons - 1 x ⅜" black or brown
- perlé thread - brown or sand

Making a Block

1. Copy foundation Units A through D.
2. Foundation piece Units A through D using mid brown for background.
3. Referring to Unit Placement diagram, join Unit A to B, then add C and finally D.

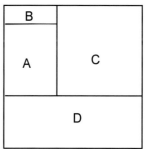

Unit Placement
(right sides facing)

4. Remove papers.

Finishing (completed after quilting)

1. Sew on button for eye.
2. Using brown or sand perlé thread, make a *plaited tail*. Attach.

Note: Your camel will look a little different to the one shown in my quilt. This one has a chest!

CAT & MOUSE

Block Size: 6" x 6" (make 2)

You will need:

- background - pale brown
- cat - black, white, ginger stripe or tan
- mouse - beige or brown
- buttons - 2 x ⅜" green, 1 x ¼" black
- perlé thread - contrasting colours

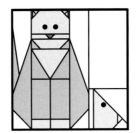

Making a Block

1. Copy foundation Units A through F, optionally making a mirrored image for the second block.
2. Using 2" fabric squares make two **folded ears** for the cat.
3. Foundation piece Unit C using pale brown for background. When adding patches 5s and 6s, remember to insert an 'ear' within each associated seam.
4. Foundation piece Units A, B, D and E using pale brown for background.
5. Referring to Unit Placement diagram, sew Units A to B, then add Unit C.

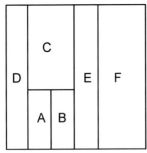

Unit Placement
(right sides facing)

6. Add Units D and E to either side.
7. Using a 1½" square make a small **folded ear** for the mouse.
8. Foundation piece Unit F using pale brown as background colour. When adding patch 4s, remember to insert the mouse's ear.
9. Add Unit F to the side of the cat.
10. Remove papers.

Finishing (completed after quilting)

1. Sew on buttons for eyes.
2. Using backstitch, embroider a mouth on the cat.
3. Using straight stitches, add some whiskers.
4. Using stem stitch, embroider a tail on the mouse.
5. Complete by sewing some mice whiskers using small straight stitches.

DOG

Block Size: 6" x 6" (Make 2)

You will need:

- background - pale green
- dog - brown, cream
- buttons - 1 x ⅜" black or brown
- perlé thread - brown

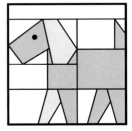

Making a Block

1. Copy foundation Units A through D.
2. Foundation piece Units A through D using pale green for background.
3. Using Unit Placement diagram, join Unit B to A, then add Unit C and finally Unit D.

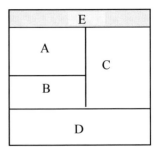

Unit Placement
(right sides facing)

4. Cut a 6½" x 1¼" strip of pale green fabric (Unit E) and sew to top of block.
5. Remove papers.

Finishing (completed after quilting)

1. Sew on buttons for eyes.
2. Using straight stitches, embroider whiskers on the dog using brown thread.

DOLPHIN

Block Size: 6" x 6" (make 2)

You will need:
- background - dark blue
- dolphin - mid grey, pale grey
- buttons -1 x ¼" black

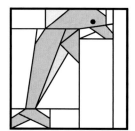

Making a Block

1. Copy foundation Units A through D, optionally making a mirrored image for the second block.
2. Foundation piece Units A through D, using dark blue fabric for background.
3. Referring to Unit Placement diagram, join Unit A to Unit B and then attach Unit C

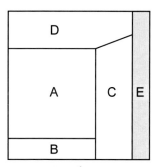

Unit Placement
(right sides facing)

4. Carefully join Unit D, taking care with the slightly angled corner.
5. Cut a 6½" x 1¼" strip of dark blue fabric (Unit E) and sew to side of dolphin block as shown.
6. Remove papers.

Finishing (completed after quilting)

1. Sew on button for eye.

DOVE & BUTTERFLY

Block Size: 6" x 6" (make 2)

You will need:
- background - pale blue
- dove - cream, pale grey, tan
- butterfly - purple, brown
- buttons - 2 x ¼" black
- perlé thread - brown

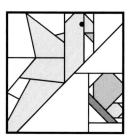

Making a Block

1. Copy foundation Units A through D, optionally making a mirrored image for the second block.
2. Foundation piece the dove using Units A, B and C, using pale blue for background.
3. Referring to Unit Placement diagram, join Unit B to Unit C and then attach to Unit A.

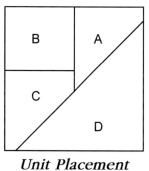

Unit Placement
(right sides facing)

4. Foundation piece the butterfly using Unit D and pale blue for background.
5. Join to dove as shown.
6. Remove papers.

Finishing (completed after quilting)

1. Sew on button for eye.
2. Using backstitch, embroider butterfly's antennae.

ELEPHANT

Block Size: 6" x 6" (make 2)

You will need:

- background - dark green
- elephant - white, 2 shades grey
- buttons - 1 x ⅜" black
- perlé thread - grey

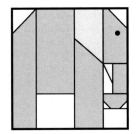

Making a Block

1. Copy foundation Units A through D.
2. Foundation piece Units A through D, using dark green for background.
3. Referring to Unit Placement diagram, join Unit A to B and then add Unit C and finally Unit D.

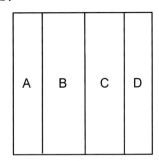

Unit Placement
(right sides facing)

4. Remove papers.

Finishing (completed after quilting)

1. Sew on button for eye.
2. Using grey perlé thread, make a ***plaited tail***. Attach.

> *Remove papers in the opposite numerical order to that used for sewing i.e. last piece first.*
>
> *This makes it much easier to remove papers fully.*

FISHES

Block Size: 6" x 6" (make 2)

You will need:

- background - dark blue
- fishes - various bright colours
- buttons - 2 x ¼" black

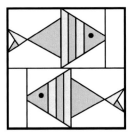

Making a Block

1. Make 2 copies of foundation Units A through C – reversing one set.
2. Foundation piece Units A through C, using dark blue fabric for background.
3. Referring to Unit placement diagrams, join Units A to their respective Units B and then attach Units C.

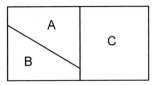

Fish Sub Unit

4. Join the two fish sub-blocks together:

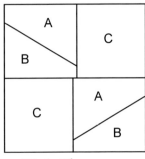

Unit Placement
(right sides facing)

5. Remove papers.

Finishing (completed after quilting)

1. Sew on buttons for eyes.

GEESE

Block Size: 6" x 6" (make 1)

You will need:
- background - mid blue
- geese - tan, 2 shades cream
- buttons - 2 x ¼" black

Making a Block

1. Make two copies of foundation Units A through C.
2. Foundation piece Units A, B and C using mid blue for background.
3. Referring to Unit Placement diagrams, join each Unit B to respective Units A and then add Units C.

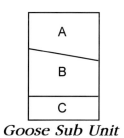

Goose Sub Unit

4. Join the two goose sub-blocks together.
5. Cut a 6½" x 2¼" strip of mid blue fabric (Unit D) and sew to top of goose sub-blocks:

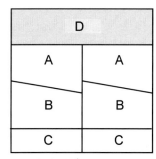

Unit Placement
(right sides facing)

6. Remove papers.

Finishing (completed after quilting)

1. Sew on buttons for eyes.

GIRAFFE

Block Size: 6" x 16" (make 2)

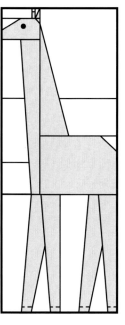

You will need:
- background - dark green, mid brown, mottled
- giraffe - blocky fabric, brown
- buttons - 1 x ⅜" black
- perlé thread - brown

Making a Block

1. Copy foundation Units A through E
2. Foundation piece Units A through E using appropriate colours for background.
3. Using Unit Placement diagram, join Unit A to B.

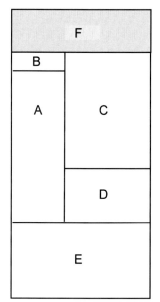

Unit Placement
(right sides facing)

4. Join Unit C to D and then join to head and neck section. Add Unit E.
5. Cut a 6½" x 2¼" strip of dark green fabric (Unit F) and sew to top of block.
6. Remove papers.

Finishing (completed after quilting)

1. Sew on button for eye.
2. Using brown perlé thread, make a *plaited tail*. Attach.

LION

Block Size: 6" x 6" (make 1)

You will need:
- background - dark green
- lion - gold, light brown, textured brown (mane)
- buttons - 2 x ⅜" brown or black
- perlé thread - brown

Making a Block

1. Copy foundation Units A through D.
2. Using 2" fabric squares make two **folded ears**.
3. Foundation piece Unit A using dark green for background. When adding patches 13s and 14s, remember to insert an 'ear' within each associated seam.
4. Foundation piece Units B, C and D using dark green for background.
5. Referring to Unit Placement diagram, join Unit A to B, then add C and finally D.

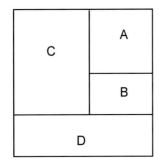

Unit Placement
(right sides facing)

6. Remove papers.

Finishing (completed after quilting)

1. Sew on buttons for eyes.
2. Using brown perlé thread, make a **plaited tail**. Attach.
3. Using backstitch, embroider a mouth.
4. Using straight stitches, add whiskers.

LIONESS

Block Size: 6" x 6" (make 1)

You will need:
- background - dark green
- lioness - gold, light brown
- buttons - 2 x ⅜" brown or black
- perlé thread - brown

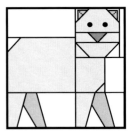

Making a Block

The Lioness is constructed in exactly the same way as the lion except that Units A through C have slightly different foundation templates.

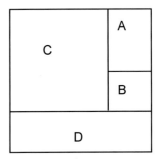

Unit Placement
(right sides facing)

Finishing (completed after quilting)

1. Sew on buttons for eyes.
2. Using brown perlé thread, make a **plaited tail**. Attach.
3. Using backstitch, embroider a mouth.
4. Using straight stitches, add whiskers.

> *Press and trim seam allowances each time a new piece is added to a block.*
>
> *This assists with ensuring accuracy and reduces unnecessary bulk.*

MRS NOAH

Block Size: 4" x 6" (make 1)

You will need:
- background - pale brown
- Mrs. Noah - pink, floral, flesh, brown
- buttons - 2 x ¼" brown or dove grey
- perlé thread - flesh, red

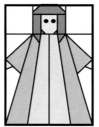

Making a Block
1. Copy foundation Units A through C.
2. Foundation piece Units A through C using pale brown fabric for background.
3. Referring to Unit Placement diagram, join Unit A to Unit B and then add Unit C.

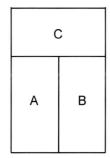

Unit Placement
(right sides facing)

4. Remove papers.

Finishing (completed after quilting)
1. Sew on buttons for eyes.
2. Using small straight stitches, embroider a nose (flesh) and mouth (red) on Mrs. Noah.

NOAH & BEES

Block Size: 6" x 6" (Make m)

You will need:
- background - pale green
- Noah - white, flesh, 2 shades of blue
- bees - black, gold, silver grey
- buttons - 4 x ¼" dove grey
- perlé thread - flesh

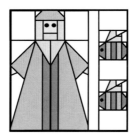

Making a Block
1. Copy foundation Units A through C and make two copies of foundation Units D through F.
2. Using pale green fabric for background, foundation piece Units A through C.
3. Referring to Unit Placement diagrams make Noah Unit by joining Unit A to Unit B and then adding Unit C (a).

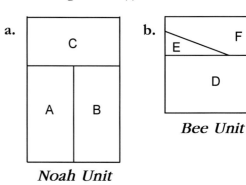

Noah Unit   **Bee Unit**

4. Foundation piece both sets of Units D, E and F, using pale green for background.
5. To make each bee, join a Unit D to Unit E and then add a Unit F (b).
6. Cut three 2" x 1½" strips of pale green fabric, Units G.
7. Join one of these to top of each bee and join the third to bottom of one bee as shown. Join bees together:

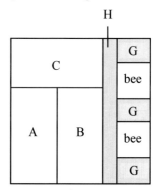

Unit Placement
(right sides facing)

8. Cut a 6½" x 1" strips of pale green fabric, Unit H. Sew this to the side of bee sub-blocks as shown:
9. Attach bees to side of Noah's sub-block.
10. Remove papers.

Finishing (completed after quilting)
1. Sew on buttons for eyes.
2. Using a small straight stitch, embroider a nose on Noah.

PENGUINS

Block Size: 6" x 6" (make 1)

You will need:
- background - mid blue
- penguins - 2 shades black, white, orange, gold
- buttons - 2 x ¼" black

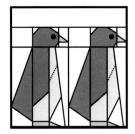

Making a Block

1. Make 2 copies of Foundation Units A through E.
2. Foundation piece Units A, B, D and E using mid blue for background.
3. Foundation piece Unit C. Either to give a penguin a colourful chest, piece 2c and 3c separately, or for a penguin without a flash use a single fabric piece covering both 2c and 3c.
4. Referring to Unit Placement diagrams, join each Unit B to their respective Units A.

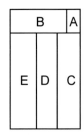

Penguin sub-block

5. Join Units C, D and E together and join to appropriate head section as above.
6. Join the two penguin sub-blocks together.
7. Cut a 6½" x 1½" strip of mid blue fabric (Unit F) and sew to top of penguin sub-blocks.

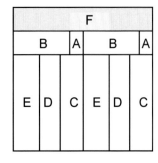

Unit Placement
(right sides facing)

8. Remove papers.

Finishing (completed after quilting)

1. Sew on buttons for eyes.

PIG

Block Size: 6" x 6" (make 2)

You will need:
- background - pale brown
- pig - black, 2 shades pink
- buttons -2 x ⅜" black, 2 x ¼" tan
- perlé thread - pink

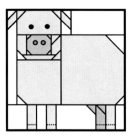

Making a Block

1. Copy Foundation Units A through E, optionally making a mirrored image for the second block.
2. Foundation piece Units A through D using pale brown for background.
3. (Optional) - To give the pig trotters, first join strips of black and pink or black and dark pink fabrics and use for pieces 2p, 4p, 7b and 9p when making Unit E.
4. Foundation piece Unit E, again using pale brown for background.
5. Referring to Unit Placement diagram, join Unit A to Unit B, attach Unit C and then Unit D.

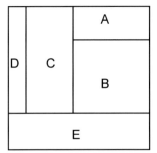

Unit Placement
(right sides facing)

6. Finally add Unit E to the bottom.
7. Remove papers.

Finishing (completed after quilting)

1. Sew on buttons for eyes and snout.
2. Using stem stitch, embroider a curly tail.

POLAR BEAR

Block Size: 6" x 6" (make 2)

You will need:
- background - mid blue
- bear - black, white
- buttons - 1 x ¼" black

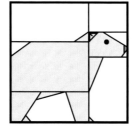

Making a Block

1. Copy Foundation Units A through E.
2. Using a 2" square of fabric make a *folded ear* for the bear.
3. Foundation piece Unit A using mid blue for background. When adding patch 3b remember to insert the 'ear' within the associated seam.
4. Foundation piece Units B through E using mid blue for background.
5. Referring to Unit Placement diagram, join Units A and B together.

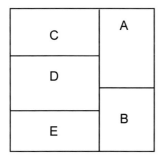

Unit Placement
(right sides facing)

6. Join Units C, D and E together and then join to head section.
7. Remove papers.

Finishing (completed after quilting)

1. Sew on button for eye.

> *Reduce the machine stitch length when foundation piecing.*
>
> *This makes it easier to remove the papers afterwards.*

RABBITS

Block Size: 6" x 6" (make 1)

You will need:
- background - mid green
- rabbits - brown, tan, pale grey
- buttons - 2 x ¼" black
- perlé thread - brown or grey

Making a Block

1. Make 2 copies of foundation Units A through D.
2. Foundation piece Units A, B and C using mid green for background.
3. Referring to Unit Placement diagrams, join each Unit B to Units A and then add Units C.
4. Finally add Units D to the top of each sub-block.

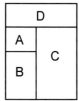

Rabbit sub-block

5. Join the two rabbit sub-blocks together.
6. Cut a 6½" x 2¼" strip of mid green fabric (Unit E) and sew this across top of sub-blocks.

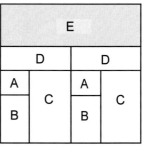

Unit Placement
(right sides facing)

7. Remove papers.

Finishing (completed after quilting)

1. Sew on buttons for eyes.
2. Using straight stitches, embroider each rabbit's whiskers.

SEA LION

Block Size: 6" x 6" (make 2)

You will need:

- background - mid blue
- sea lion - 2 shades grey/purple grey
- buttons - 1 x ⅜" black
- perlé thread - grey

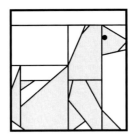

Making a Block

1. Copy foundation Units A through C.
2. Foundation piece Units A through C using mid blue for background.
3. Referring to Unit Placement diagram, join Unit A to Unit B and then attach Unit C.

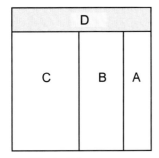

Unit Placement
(right sides facing)

4. Cut a 6½" x 1¼" strip of mid blue fabric (Unit D) and sew to top of block.
5. Remove papers.

Finishing (completed after quilting)

1. Sew on button for eye.
2. Using small straight stitches, embroider whiskers and optionally a nose.

> *Audition unusual fabrics as possible candidates for inclusion in blocks.*
>
> *Only small scraps are needed - are there any interesting textures that can be incorporated?*

SHEEP

Block Size: 6" x 6" (make 2)

You will need:

- background - mid green
- sheep - curly 'wool', black, cream
- buttons - 2 x ⅜" black

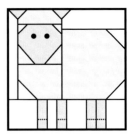

Making a Block

1. Copy Foundation Units A through D.
2. Foundation piece Units A through C using mid green for background.
3. (Optional) - To give the sheep 'feet' first join strips of black and cream fabric and use for pieces 2b, 3b, 5b and 7b when making Unit D.
4. Foundation piece Unit D.
5. Referring to Unit Placement diagram, join Units A and C to either side of Unit B.

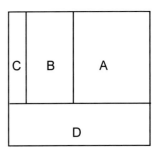

Unit Placement
(right sides facing)

6. Finally add Unit D to the bottom.
7. Remove papers.

Finishing (completed after quilting)

1. Sew on buttons for eyes.

SNAKES & SNAILS

Block Size: 6" x 6" (make 1)

You will need:
- background - pale brown
- snakes - spotty
- snails - marbled, grey
- buttons - 2 x ¼" black, 2 x ¼" tan
- perlé thread - grey, sand

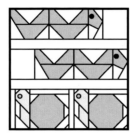

Making a Block
1. Make 2 copies of foundation Units A through E.
2. Foundation piece both snails using Units A and B and pale brown fabric for background.
3. Referring to Unit Placement diagram, join each Unit A to Unit B and then join the 2 snails together.

Snail sub-block

4. Foundation piece both snakes using Units C, D and Unit E and pale brown for background.
5. Referring to Unit Placement diagram below, join Units C and E to either side of Unit D - repeat for both snakes.
6. Cut two 1¾" x 2" strips of beige fabric, Units F. Sew one to front of first snake and the other to back of second snake.

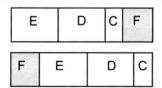

Snake sub-blocks

7. Cut two 6½" x 1" strips of beige fabric, Units G and sew one to bottom of each snake block.
8. Attach snails to bottom of snake section.

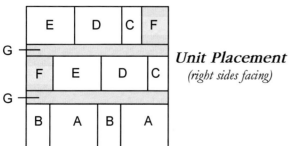

Unit Placement
(right sides facing)

9. Remove papers.

Finishing (completed after quilting)
1. Sew on buttons for eyes.
2. Using backstitch, embroider snails' feelers, adding a French knot at the ends.
3. Using backstitch and a complimentary shade of perlé thread, embroider a spiral onto each snail's shell.

WHALE

Block Size: 6" x 6" (make 2)

You will need:
- background - dark blue
- whale - grey blue, pale grey
- buttons - 1 x ⅜" black
- perlé thread - white

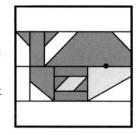

Making a Block
1. Copy Foundation Units A through C, optionally making a mirrored image for the second block.
2. Foundation piece Units A through C, using dark blue fabric for background.
3. Referring to Unit Placement diagram, join Unit A to Unit B and then attach Unit C.

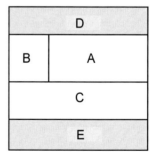

Unit Placement
(right sides facing)

4. Cut 2, 6½" x 1¾" strips of dark blue fabric (Units D and E) and sew these to the top and bottom of the whale sub-block.
5. Remove papers.

Finishing (completed after quilting)
1. Sew on button for eye.
2. Using backstitch, embroider a water spout.

ZEBRA

Block Size: 6" x 6" (make 2)

You will need:

- background - mid brown
- zebra - black/white stripe, black
- buttons - 1 x ⅜" black
- perlé thread - black

Making a Block

1. Copy Foundation Units A through D.
2. Foundation piece Units A through C using mid brown for background.
3. (Optional) - To give the zebra 'hooves' first join strips of black and striped fabric and use this for pieces 2z, 4z, 6z and 8z when making Unit D.
4. Foundation piece Unit D.
5. Using Unit Placement diagram, join Unit A to B, then add Unit C and finally Unit D.

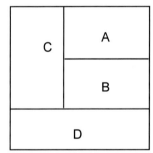

Unit Placement
(right sides facing)

6. Remove papers.

Finishing (completed after quilting)

1. Sew on button for eye.
2. Using black perlé thread, make a ***tassel tail***. Attach.

ARK ROOF

Block Size: 24" x 7" (Make 1)

You will need:

- roof - pale blue, mid & dark brown, red

Making a Block

1. From pale blue fabric cut two rectangles of fabric, each 10¾" x 7½".

2. From mid brown cut two rectangles of fabric, each 10¾" x 6¼".
3. From red fabric cut a 3½" x 24½" strip.
4. From dark brown cut 7½" x 4" chimney strip.
5. With pencil, mark a diagonal line across the back of one mid brown rectangle from top right to bottom left corner.
6. Draw a parallel line ¼" above first pencil line creating a seam allowance.
7. Cut along this line. Discard smaller piece of fabric.

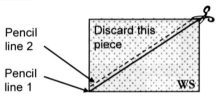

8. Fold seam allowance to wrong side and press.
9. With right sides facing upwards match right-angled corner of triangle to corresponding corner of a blue rectangle.

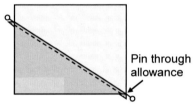

10. Pin each end of diagonal (triangle's hypotenuse), putting pins through just the seam allowance.

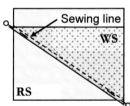

11. Flip triangle up. Stitch. Fold back down. Remove pins. Trim 'ears'. Press.

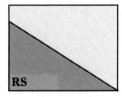

Finished

12. Repeat with other pair of rectangles, but draw the diagonal line from top left to bottom right.
13. Join roof sections to chimney, attach red strip to the bottom as shown on page 6.

All aboard the Ark ...

Down in the depths ...

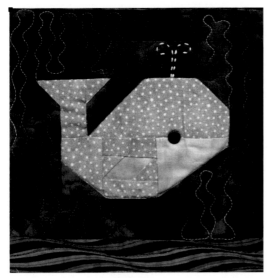

Whale 1

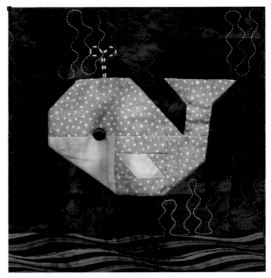

Whale 2

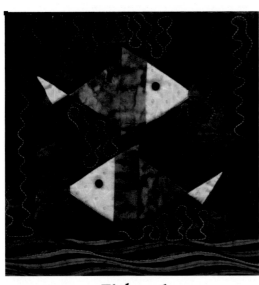

Fishes 1

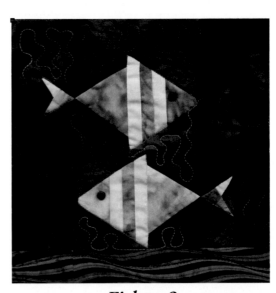

Fishes 2

Dolphin 1

Dolphin 2

From those Icy Places ...

Polar Bear 1

Polar Bear 2

Penguins

Geese

Sea Lion 1

Sea Lion 2

27

Already Aboard and Ready to Sail ...

Pig 1

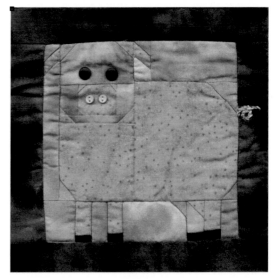

Pig 2

Snakes & Snails

Mrs Noah

Cat & Mouse 1

Cat & Mouse 2

Down at the Farm ...

Sheep 1

Sheep 2

Rabbits

Noah & Bees

Dog 1

Dog 2

On Safari ...

Lion

Lioness

Giraffe 1

Giraffe 2

Zebra 1

Zebra 2

Elephant 1

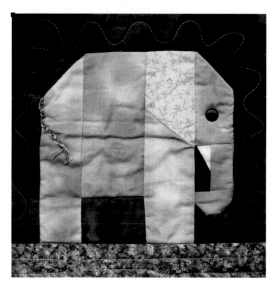

Elephant 2

Too hot to handle!

Camel 1

Camel 2

Flying High!

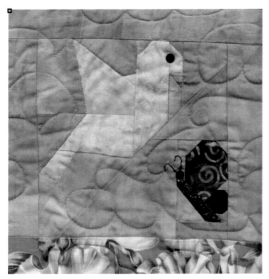

Dove & Butterfly 1

Dove & Butterfly 2

Bats

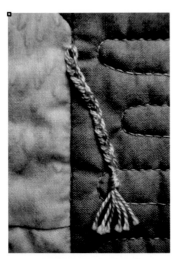

Plaited Tail

Tassel Tail

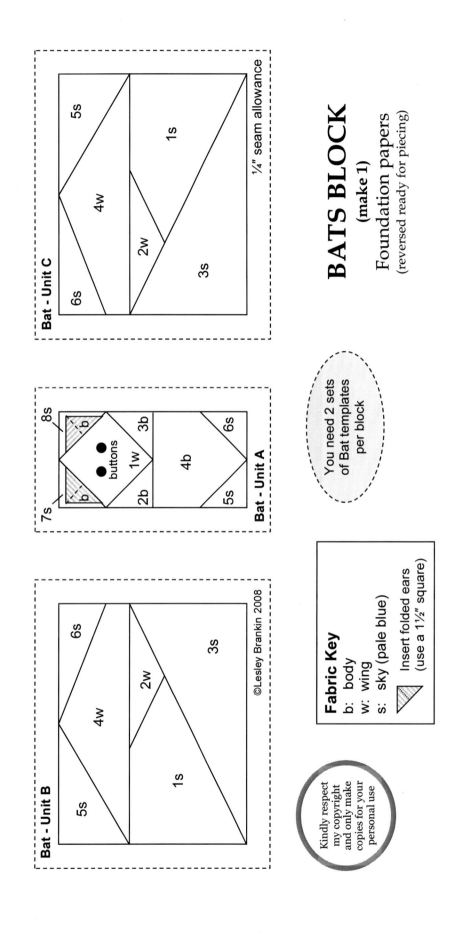

BATS BLOCK
(make 1)
Foundation papers
(reversed ready for piecing)

Bat - Unit C

5s · 1s · 4w · 2w · 6s · 3s

¼" seam allowance

Bat - Unit A

8s · b · 3b · 1w · buttons · 6s · 4b · 2b · 5s · 7s · b

You need 2 sets of Bat templates per block

Bat - Unit B

6s · 3s · 4w · 2w · 5s · 1s

©Lesley Brankin 2008

Fabric Key
b: body
w: wing
s: sky (pale blue)
Insert folded ears (use a 1½" square)

33

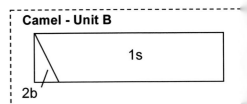

Camel - Unit B

1s

2b

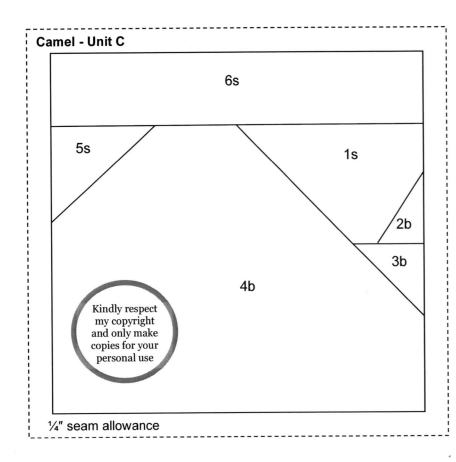

Camel - Unit C

6s

5s

1s

2b

3b

4b

Kindly respect my copyright and only make copies for your personal use

¼" seam allowance

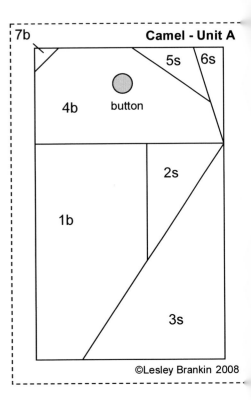

7b

Camel - Unit A

5s

6s

4b

button

2s

1b

3s

©Lesley Brankin 2008

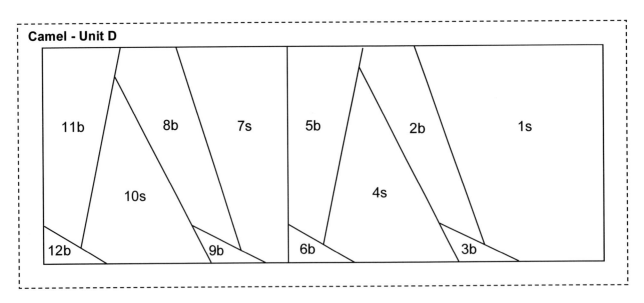

Camel - Unit D

11b

8b

7s

5b

2b

1s

10s

4s

12b

9b

6b

3b

CAMEL BLOCK

(Make 2)

Foundation papers

(reversed ready for piecing)

Fabric Key

b: body

s: sky (mid brown)

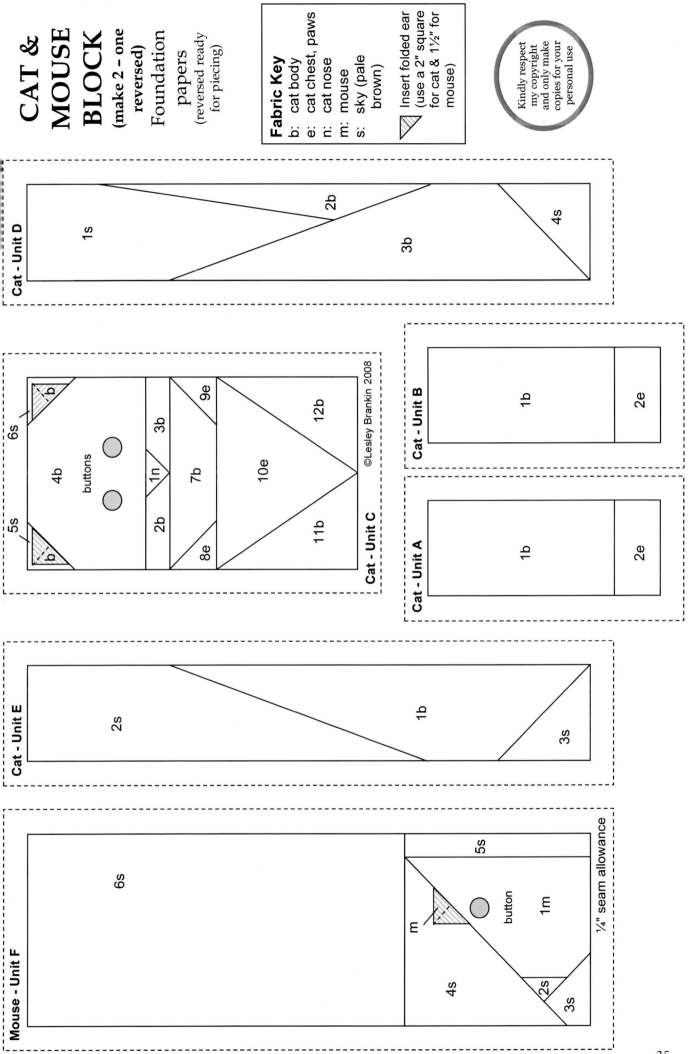

CAT & MOUSE BLOCK

(make 2 – one reversed) Foundation papers (reversed ready for piecing)

Fabric Key
b: cat body
e: cat chest, paws
n: cat nose
m: mouse
s: sky (pale brown)

Insert folded ear (use a 2" square for cat & 1½" for mouse)

Kindly respect my copyright and only make copies for your personal use

Cat - Unit D
1s
2b
3b
4s

Cat - Unit C
6s   b
5s   b
4b
buttons
5s
2b   1n   3b
8e   7b   9e
11b 10e 12b
©Lesley Brankin 2008

Cat - Unit B
1b
2e

Cat - Unit A
1b
2e

Cat - Unit E
2s
1b
3s

Mouse - Unit F
6s
5s
m
4s
button
1m
2s
3s
¼" seam allowance

35

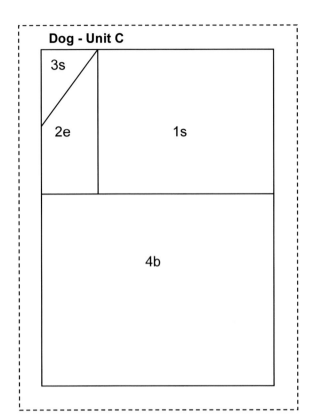

Dog - Unit C

3s
2e
1s
4b

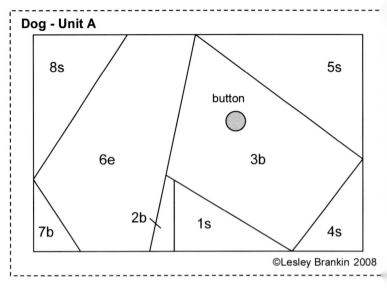

Dog - Unit A

8s
5s
button
6e
3b
7b
2b
1s
4s

©Lesley Brankin 2008

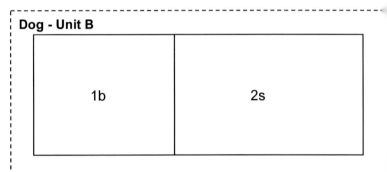

Dog - Unit B

1b
2s

DOG BLOCK

(make 2)
Foundation papers
(reversed ready for piecing)

Fabric Key
b: body
e: ear/tail
s: sky (pale green)

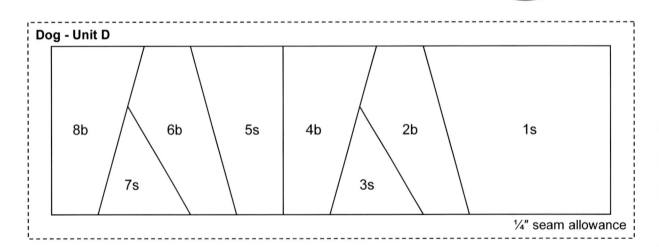

Dog - Unit D

8b
6b
5s
4b
2b
1s
7s
3s

¼″ seam allowance

36

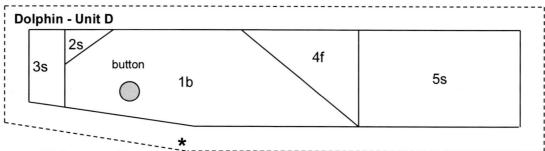

Dolphin - Unit D

3s · 2s · button · 1b · 4f · 5s

*

*Take care with
angled corner – sew
as two seams*

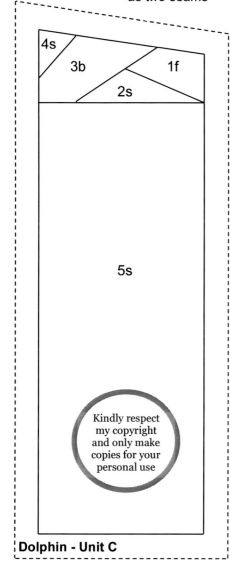

Dolphin - Unit C

4s · 3b · 1f · 2s · 5s

Kindly respect
my copyright
and only make
copies for your
personal use

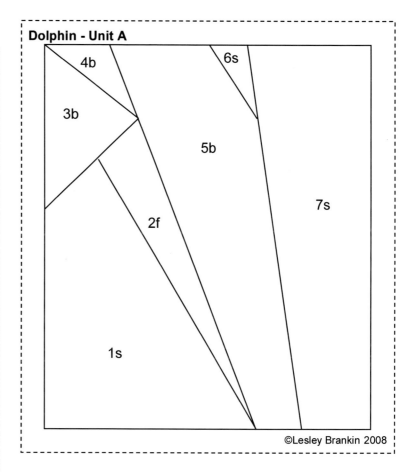

Dolphin - Unit A

4b · 6s · 3b · 5b · 7s · 2f · 1s

©Lesley Brankin 2008

Dolphin - Unit B

6s · 5s · 3b · 4s · 2b · 1s

¼" seam allowance

DOLPHIN BLOCK

(make 2 – one reversed)

Foundation papers

(reversed ready for piecing)

Fabric Key

b: body
f: fin, lower body
s: sea (dark blue)

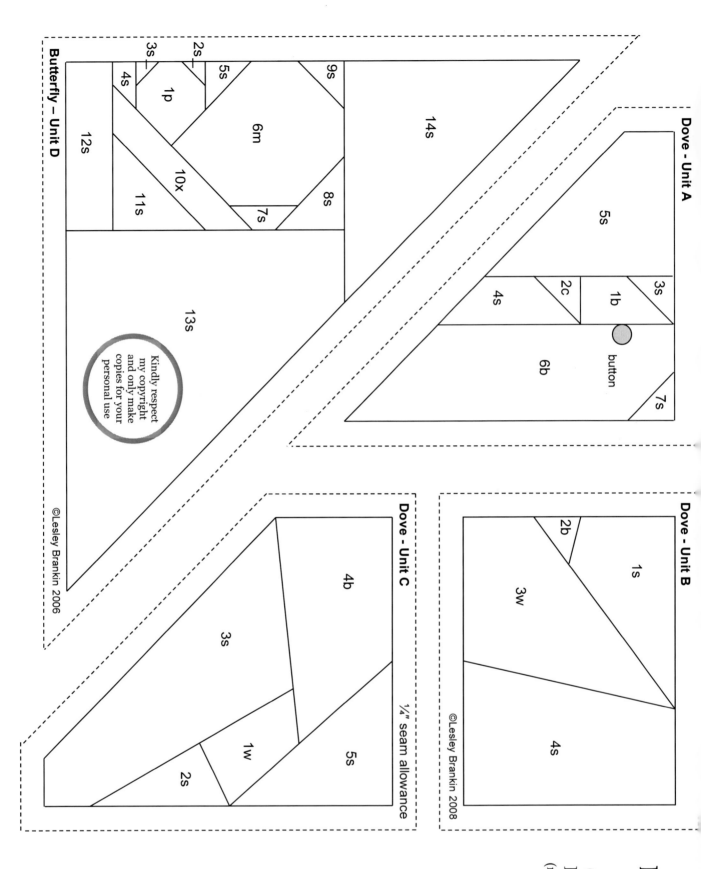

DOVE & BUTTERFLY BLOCK

(make 2 – 1 reversed)

Foundation papers

(reversed ready for piecing)

Dove - Unit A

Dove - Unit B

©Lesley Brankin 2008

Dove - Unit C

¼" seam allowance

Butterfly – Unit D

©Lesley Brankin 2006

Kindly respect my copyright and only make copies for your personal use

Fabric Key

s: sky (pale blue)

bird:
b: body
c: bill
w: wing

butterfly:
x: body
m: wing fabric 1
p: wing fabric 2

ELEPHANT BLOCK

(make 2)

Foundation papers
(reversed ready for piecing)

Fabric Key
- b: body
- t: tusk
- e: ear
- s: sky (dark green)

Elephant - Unit A

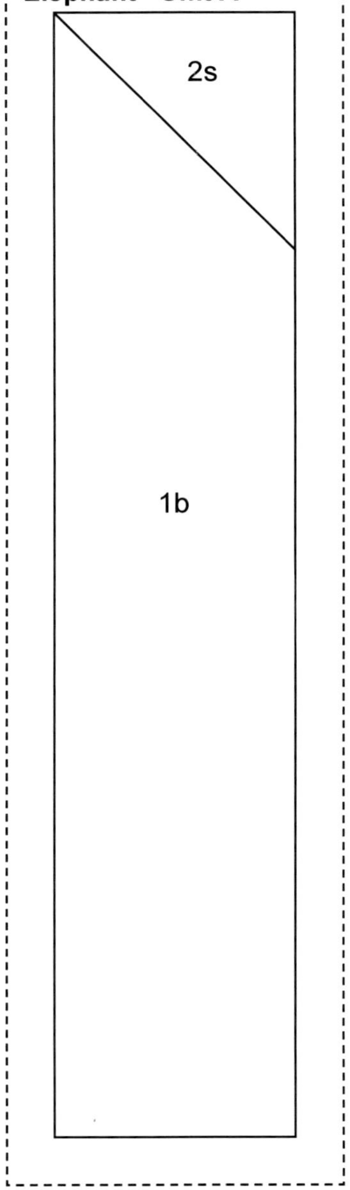

2s

1b

Elephant - Unit B

2b

1s

¼" seam allowance

Elephant - Unit C

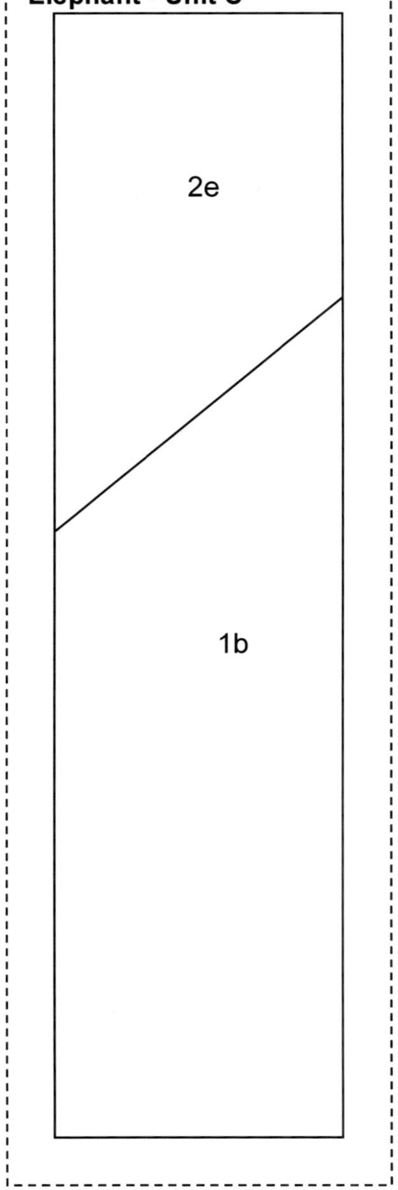

2e

1b

Elephant - Unit D

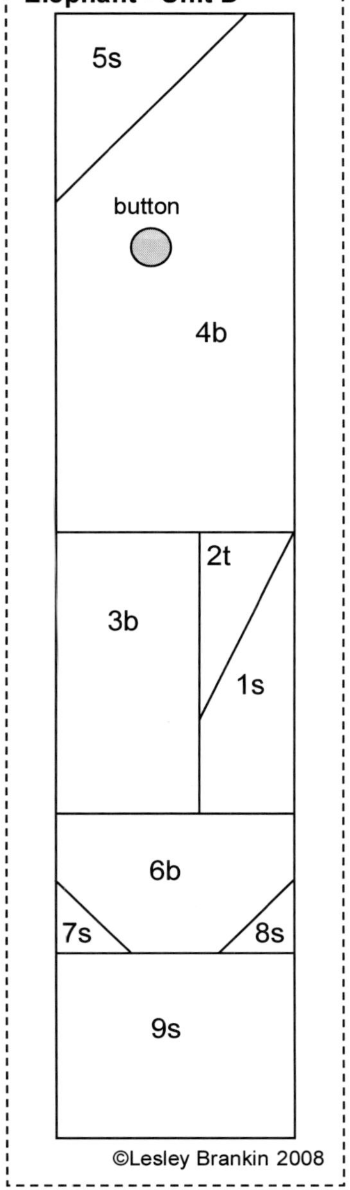

5s

button

4b

2t

1s

3b

6b

8s

7s

9s

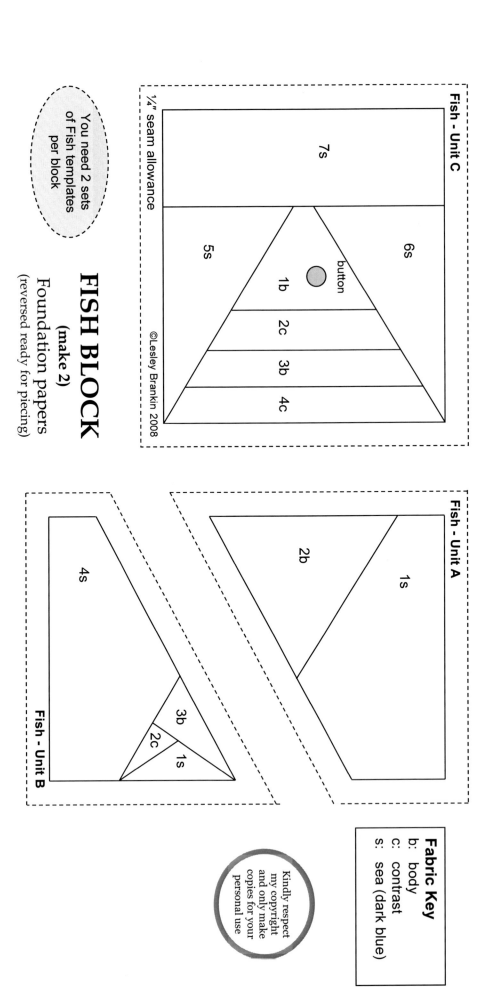

FISH BLOCK
(make 2)
Foundation papers
(reversed ready for piecing)

You need 2 sets of Fish templates per block

¼" seam allowance

©Lesley Brankin 2008

Fish - Unit C

7s

5s

6s

button

1b

2c

3b

4c

Fish - Unit A

2b

1s

Fish - Unit B

4s

3b

2c

1s

Fabric Key
b: body
c: contrast
s: sea (dark blue)

GEESE BLOCK

(make 1)
Foundation papers
(reversed ready for piecing)

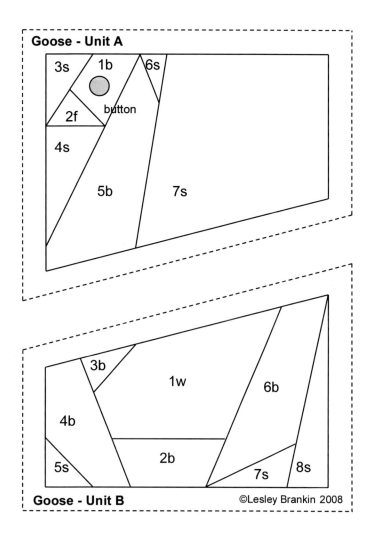

Goose - Unit A

3s | 1b | 6s
button
2f
4s
5b | 7s

Goose - Unit B

3b
1w
6b
4b
5s | 2b | 7s | 8s

©Lesley Brankin 2008

Fabric Key	
b:	body
r:	wing
f:	feet/bill
s:	sky (mid blue)

You need 2 sets
of Geese templates
per block

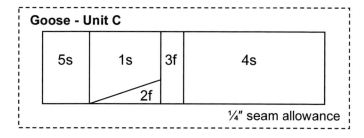

Goose - Unit C

5s | 1s | 3f | 4s
2f

¼" seam allowance

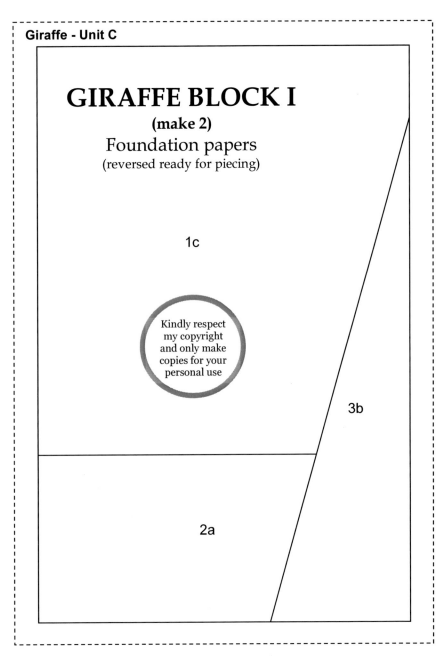

Giraffe - Unit C

GIRAFFE BLOCK I
(make 2)
Foundation papers
(reversed ready for piecing)

1c

3b

2a

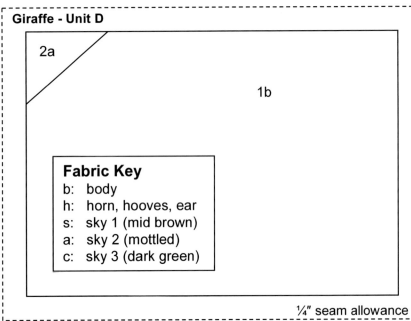

Giraffe - Unit D

2a

1b

Fabric Key
b: body
h: horn, hooves, ear
s: sky 1 (mid brown)
a: sky 2 (mottled)
c: sky 3 (dark green)

¼″ seam allowance

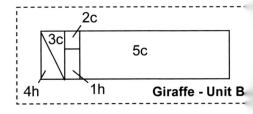

2c

3c

5c

4h   1h   **Giraffe - Unit B**

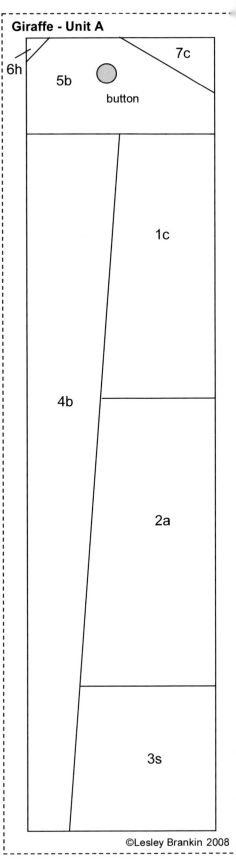

Giraffe - Unit A

6h   5b   button   7c

1c

4b

2a

3s

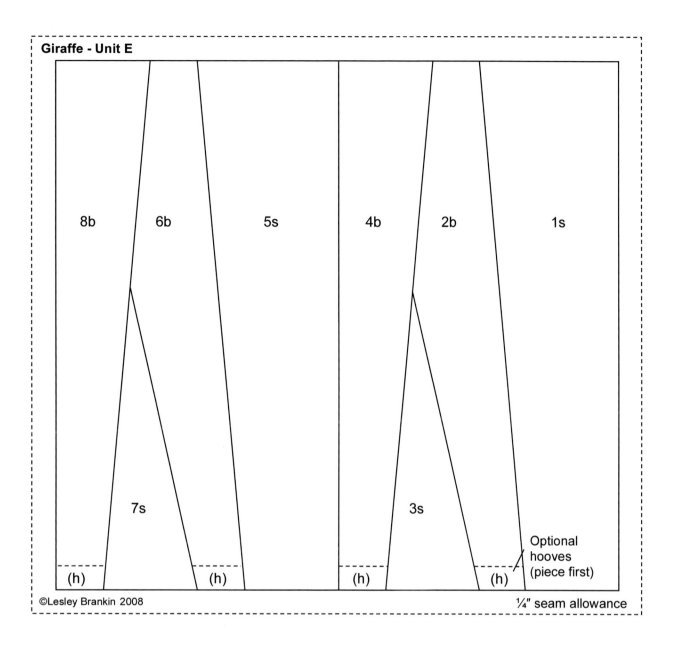

GIRAFFE BLOCK II

(make 2)

Foundation papers

(reversed ready for piecing)

Fabric Key
b: body
h: horn, hooves, ear
s: sky 1 (mid brown)
a: sky 2 (mottled)
c: sky 3 (dark green)

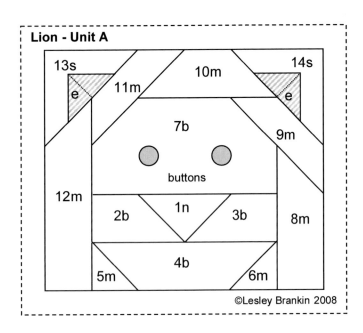

Lion - Unit A

13s
14s
e
e
11m
10m
7b
9m
buttons
12m
2b · 1n · 3b
8m
4b
5m · 6m

©Lesley Brankin 2008

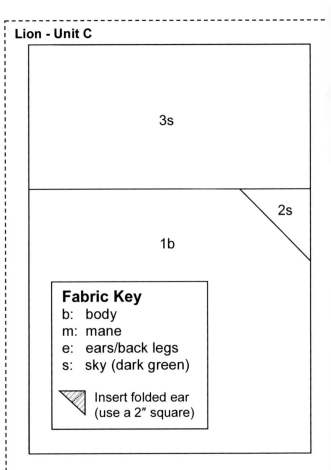

Lion - Unit C

3s

2s

1b

Fabric Key
b: body
m: mane
e: ears/back legs
s: sky (dark green)

Insert folded ear
(use a 2″ square)

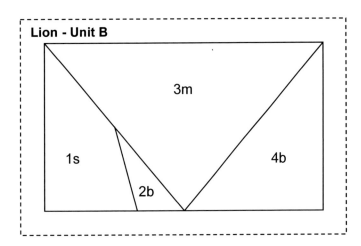

Lion - Unit B

3m

1s

2b

4b

LION BLOCK
(make 1)
Foundation papers
(reversed ready for piecing)

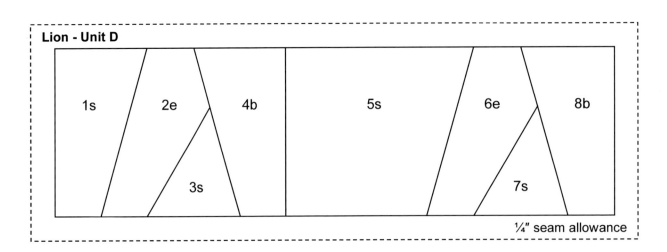

Lion - Unit D

1s · 2e · 4b
3s
5s · 6e · 8b
7s

¼″ seam allowance

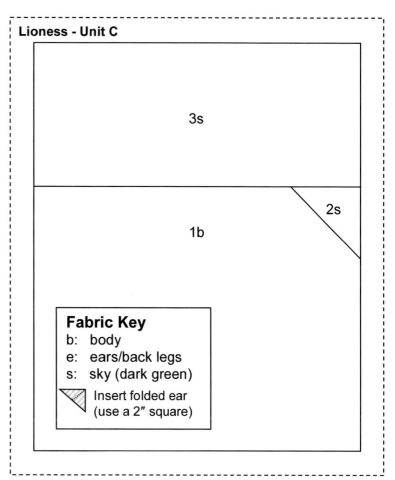

Lioness - Unit C

3s

1b

2s

Fabric Key
b: body
e: ears/back legs
s: sky (dark green)

Insert folded ear
(use a 2″ square)

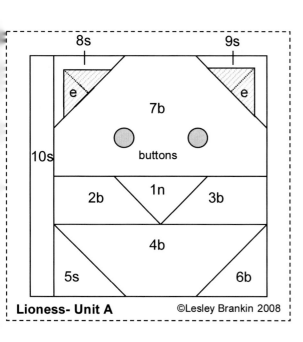

Lioness- Unit A

8s   9s

e   e

7b

buttons

10s

2b   1n   3b

4b

5s   6b

©Lesley Brankin 2008

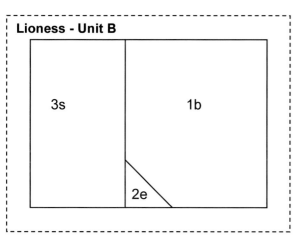

Lioness - Unit B

3s   1b

2e

Kindly respect
my copyright
and only make
copies for your
personal use

LIONESS BLOCK
(make 1)
Foundation papers
(reversed ready for piecing)

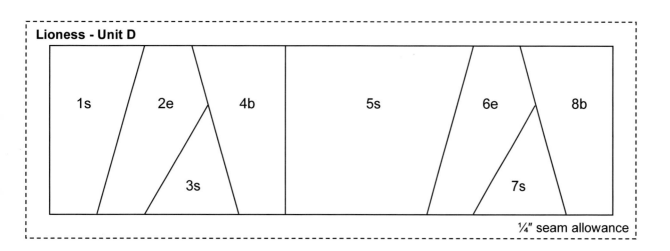

Lioness - Unit D

1s   2e   4b   5s   6e   8b

3s   7s

¼″ seam allowance

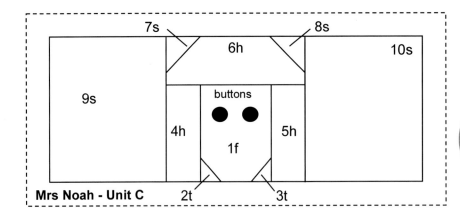

Mrs Noah - Unit C

- 7s
- 8s
- 6h
- 10s
- 9s
- buttons
- 4h
- 1f
- 5h
- 2t
- 3t

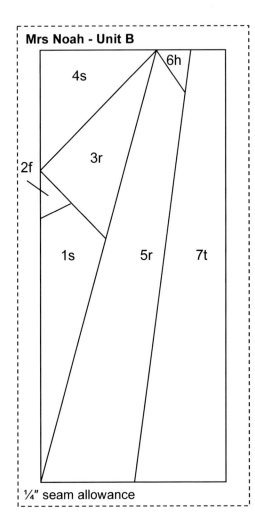

Mrs Noah - Unit B

- 4s
- 6h
- 2f
- 3r
- 1s
- 5r
- 7t

¼" seam allowance

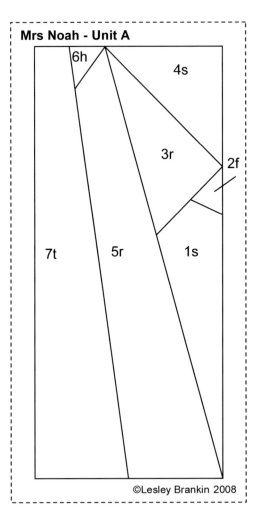

Mrs Noah - Unit A

- 6h
- 4s
- 3r
- 2f
- 7t
- 5r
- 1s

Fabric Key	
h:	hair
r:	robe
f:	face /hands
t:	trim
s:	sky (pale brown)

MRS NOAH BLOCK

(make 1)

Foundation papers

(reversed ready for piecing)

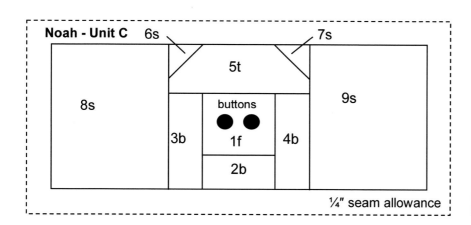

Noah - Unit C

6s 7s

5t

8s buttons 9s

3b 1f 4b

2b

¼" seam allowance

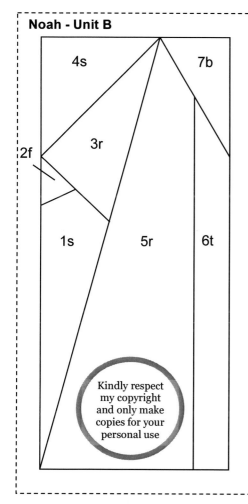

Noah - Unit B

4s 7b

2f 3r

1s 5r 6t

Kindly respect
my copyright
and only make
copies for your
personal use

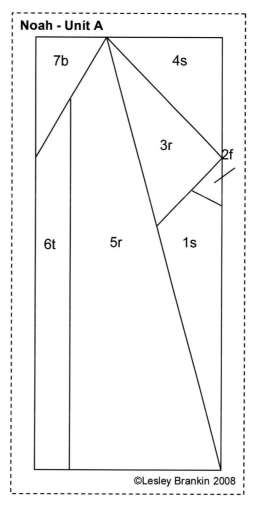

Noah - Unit A

7b 4s

3r 2f

6t 5r 1s

©Lesley Brankin 2008

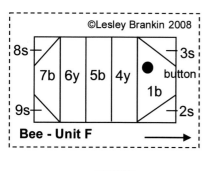

©Lesley Brankin 2008

8s 3s

7b 6y 5b 4y button

1b

9s 2s

Bee - Unit F →

You need 2 sets
of Bee templates
per block

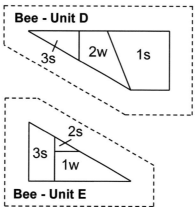

Bee - Unit D

3s 2w 1s

2s

3s 1w

Bee - Unit E

NOAH & BEES
BLOCK
(make 1)
Foundation papers
(reversed ready for piecing)

PENGUINS BLOCK
(make 1)
Foundation papers
(reversed ready for piecing)

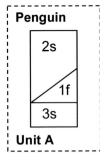

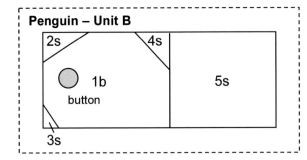

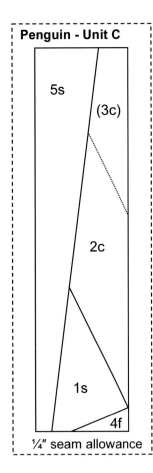

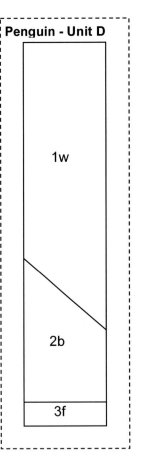

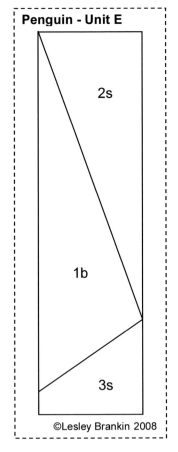

Fabric Key
b: body
f: feet, beak
c: chest/chest 2
w: wing
s: sky (mid blue)

You need 2 sets of Penguin templates per block

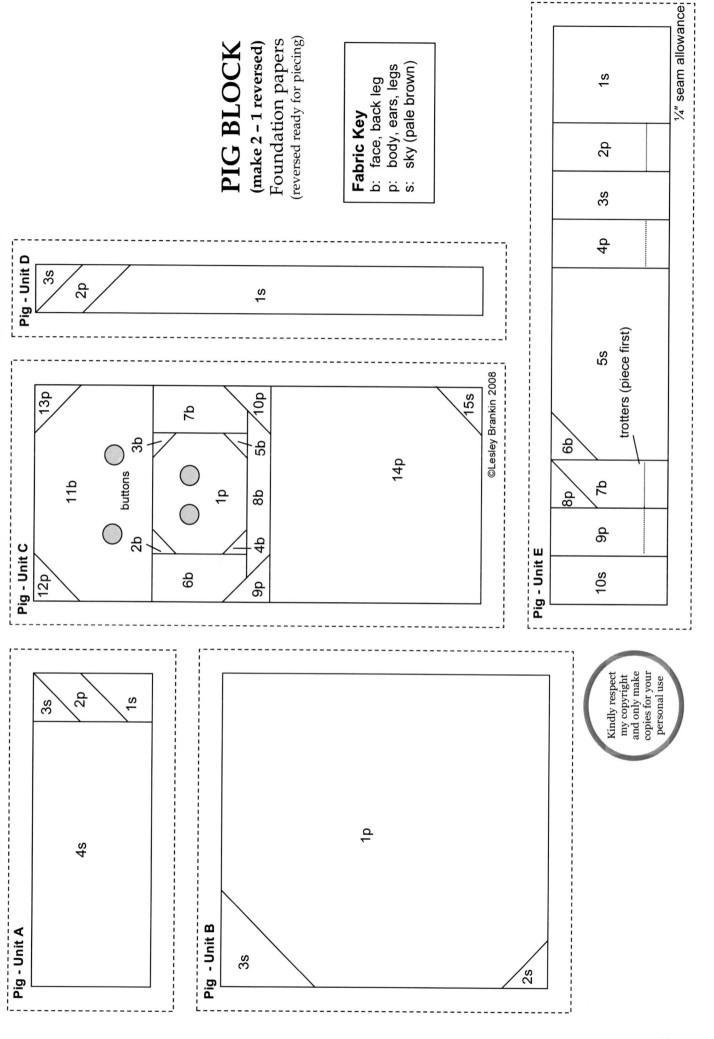

PIG BLOCK

(make 2 – 1 reversed)
Foundation papers
(reversed ready for piecing)

Fabric Key
b: face, back leg
p: body, ears, legs
s: sky (pale brown)

©Lesley Brankin 2008

Pig - Unit A

4s

3s
2p
1s

Pig - Unit B

1p

3s

2s

Pig - Unit C

13p
12p
11b
buttons
3b
2b
7b
5b
1p
8b
4b
6b
10p
9p
14p
15s

Pig - Unit D

3s
2p
1s

Pig - Unit E

1s
2p
3s
4p
5s
trotters (piece first)
6b
8p
7b
9p
10s

¼" seam allowance

49

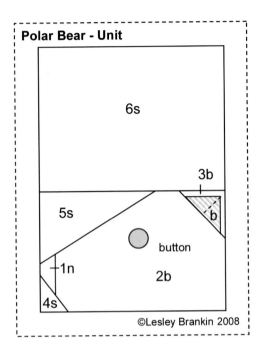

Polar Bear - Unit

6s

3b

5s

b

button

1n

2b

4s

©Lesley Brankin 2008

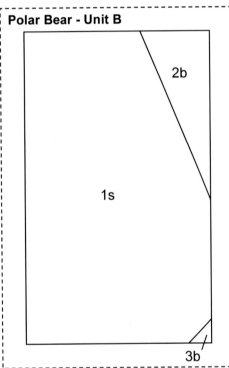

Polar Bear - Unit B

2b

1s

3b

POLAR BEAR BLOCK

(make 2)

Foundation papers
(reversed ready for piecing)

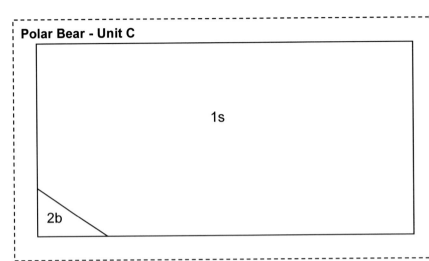

Polar Bear - Unit C

1s

2b

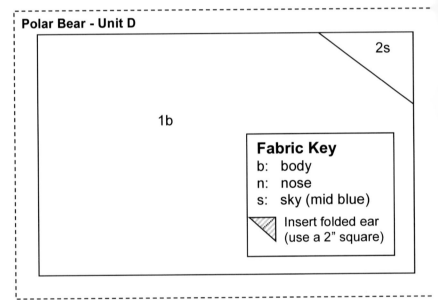

Polar Bear - Unit D

2s

1b

Fabric Key
b: body
n: nose
s: sky (mid blue)

Insert folded ear
(use a 2" square)

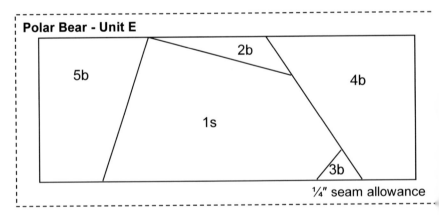

Polar Bear - Unit E

5b

2b

4b

1s

3b

¼" seam allowance

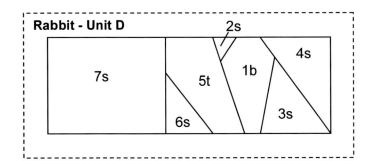

Rabbit - Unit D

2s
4s
7s
5t
1b
6s
3s

Fabric Key
b: body
t: tail/ear/foot
s: sky (mid green)

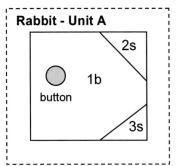

Rabbit - Unit A

2s
button
1b
3s

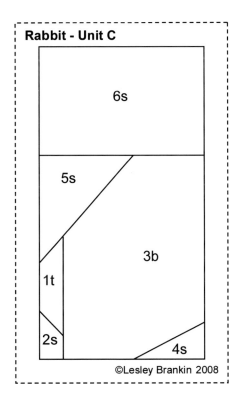

Rabbit - Unit C

6s
5s
3b
1t
2s
4s
©Lesley Brankin 2008

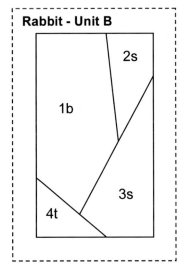

Rabbit - Unit B

2s
1b
3s
4t

RABBITS BLOCK
(make 1)
Foundation papers
(reversed ready for piecing)

You need 2 sets
of Rabbit templates
per block

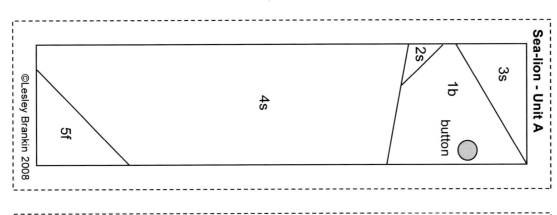

Sea-lion - Unit A

3s
2s
1b
button
4s
5f

©Lesley Brankin 2008

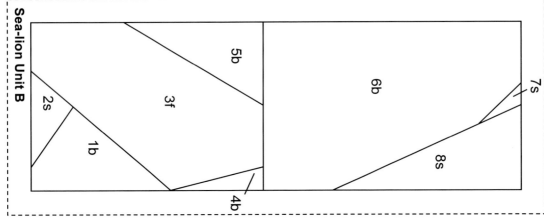

Sea-lion Unit B

5b
3f
2s
1b
4b
6b
7s
8s

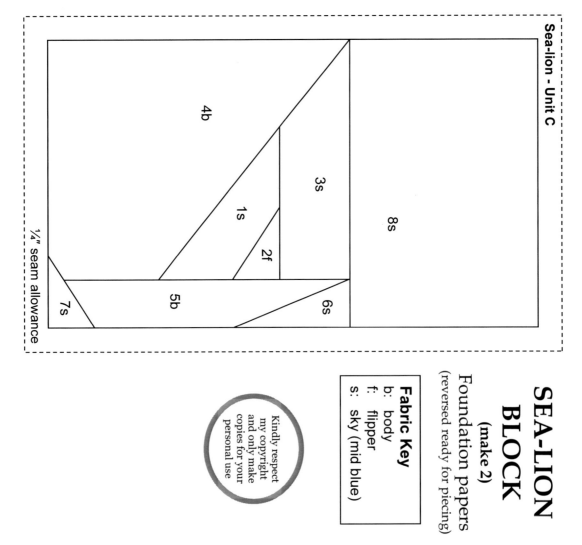

Sea-lion - Unit C

4b
3s
1s
2f
8s
5b
6s
7s

¼" seam allowance

SEA-LION
BLOCK
(make 2)

Foundation papers
(reversed ready for piecing)

Fabric Key

b: body
f: flipper
s: sky (mid blue)